THE
KITTENS *of* BOXVILLE

Text copyright © 2009 by Tracy Sunrize Johnson.
Photographs copyright © 2009 by Yoneo Morita and Ryosuke Handa.
All rights reserved. No part of this book may be reproduced in any form
without written permission from the publisher.

Library of Congress Cataloging-in-Publication Data available.

ISBN: 978-0-8118-6688-0

Manufactured in China

Designed by Tracy Sunrize Johnson.
Original concept and cardboard house design by Ryosuke Handa.
Photographs taken by Yoneo Morita.

10 9 8 7 6 5 4 3 2 1

Chronicle Books LLC
680 Second Street
San Francisco, California 94107

www.chroniclebooks.com

THE
KITTENS *of* BOXVILLE

original story by RYOSUKE HANDA

photographs by YONEO MORITA

text by TRACY SUNRIZE JOHNSON

CHRONICLE BOOKS

SAN FRANCISCO

WELCOME!!

At last you have discovered the fair seaside village of Boxville Sur la Mer! I see that you, like so many before you, wear upon your face a look of wonder and disbelief. I understand: It seems impossible that a town so cute could possibly be real. It defies all logic of reality, which so frequently is un-cute! But do not disregard this vision! Boxville Sur la Mer *is* real, and here are the pictures to prove it.

This adorable wonderland was no accident of city planning. For centuries, cat scholars sat on the sea cliffs with their furry brows knitted in concentration, chewing on the challenge of how to build a functional cat utopia. Is a river of milk possible? Is it ethical to outlaw dogs, or should dogs merely be encouraged to keep a wide berth? Many grand designs were considered and discarded by the founding forecats of the town, but one idea stands out above all the rest, as you shall quickly understand.

Indeed, Boxville Sur la Mer is a remarkable place not only because it is a fine community for kitten families, young kitten singles, and all manner of professional kitten types. There is something else about the town that is very special—and I am not speaking of the rare and elusive cloudfish, which, it is rumored, is a most especially delicious fish, found only in the skies that hover above this fantastic place.

Finally you have grasped my meaning! The main thing to notice about this place is its unique architecture: *Boxville Sur la Mer is the first and only all-kitten city where each house is made from a cutely painted cardboard box.* It's true! Prized for its unmatched properties of coziness, bitableness, and climbableness, cardboard has long been the building material of choice for kitten carpenters. As Boxville Sur la Mer plainly illustrates, cardboard also proves very versatile, suitable for all styles of homes, farmhouses, schools, and even our notable and impressive aquarium filled with many strange fish!

If you are here for the day only, certainly you will not have time to meet and marvel at every kitten in Boxville Sur la Mer, nor to admire each impressive feat of cardboard construction. But I hope a small tour will convince you that the dream you have nurtured for years is real: kitties *do* live blissfully in cardboard houses beside the ocean. My best advice to you is to travel with a friendly local kitten as he rambles through his day; this is the best way to see the city, and you will probably get to take a lot of naps, too. Every kitten who lives here is nice and cute, and would make an excellent city guide—so just step inside, and see who is awake and ready to play!

THREE'S company

HEY, UN-ARCH THAT EYEBROW! There's nothing fishy going on in this converted carriage house at the east end of Boxville Sur la Mer. Behind those blue shutters are Greta the Gray Tabby, Minnie the Maine Coon, and Boris the Russian Blue—and they're *just good friends.* Sure, they all sleep together in a soft, fluffy pile. But you would, too, if your roommates were kittens!

Boris is usually the first one awake. After a full-fat latte, some enviable stretches, and a few quick gnaws of the windowsill, he's ready to start his day; a peek out his front door proves that no rain clouds or bothersome hounds are poised to sully his good time.

"Well," sniffs Boris, nodding assertively. "Off I go then for a quick scamper . . ."*

Note: Though ever mindful of maintaining good cardiovascular health, kittens do not go jogging or running but prefer instead to go scampering.

Greta and Minnie like to sleep late. When the sun is high, they roll out of bed at last and lean out the windows to blink in the breeze and call out to their roommate:

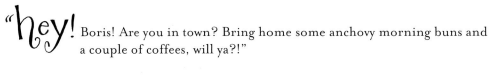

"hey! Boris! Are you in town? Bring home some anchovy morning buns and a couple of coffees, will ya?!"

"Heavy cream," Minnie adds sleepily.

When Boris returns home (without coffee or buns), he is annoyed to discover his two roommates asleep again, happily purring in the front hall. "Lazy girls!" Boris sputters, running outside and banging the shutters closed to make a ruckus and wake the household. "Get up!!" he yells. "It's a beautiful day! I'm going now to the roof of the château to look for delicious birds. Don't you want to come?"

Greta opens one eye, halfway, and lifts her head, halfway. She murmurs to Boris in the doorway, "Did you bring the coffee…?"

"No!" he shouts, "No coffee! They were out of coffee. Now come on, let's go!"

"No coffee?! You know I can't function without a decent breakfast!" Greta the Gray Tabby reaches out to box her roommate's ears, and I don't think any reasonable person would say she is out of line.

"All right! That's enough," says Boris, feeling slightly dizzy.
He scoots away from Greta and starts toward the château.
"Are you ready? Come on! We'll get coffee on the way."

"You always say that," says Greta. "And we never do."

"But maybe we should have a nap first," suggests Minnie the Maine Coon, still sprawled in her front hall. She yawns and explains: "If we are well rested, we'll probably be better at spotting those delicious birds from the roof of the château . . . Don't you think?"

"I guess so," grumbles Boris, but he is secretly glad, and he comes back inside to his cozy cardboard bedroom, takes one last sniff of the late morning air, closes his shutters, and sleeps until noon, as kittens do.

château CHATON*

WHEN BORIS AND HIS ROOMMATES AWAKE from their mid-morning nap, they spend several minutes together in the living room, blinking and yawning and swatting at each other's flicking tails. At last Boris springs into the air and cries, "The château! Remember? Birds! We'll find them! Let's go!!"

The sweet French cottage down the block is home to a serene Chartreux named Laurent, and although Laurent is a gentle, generous host, he is hardly ever home to greet visitors. "Probably out hunting," mutters Boris, scaling the back wall of Laurent's house. "That one is always hunting."

Greta and Minnie sniff around the kitchen door. "Those French really know how to cook," Minnie whispers to her roommate. "Maybe he left some *pain perdu* or a nice *croque-madame* for us on the breakfast table, hmm?"

"And some coffee," nods Greta, licking her lips. "French coffee is so delicious."

Boris, alone on the roof, is irritated. "There are no birds up here!" he yells down to the girls. "Are you listening? Hey!" But the girls are sniffing around the French country kitchen and they don't answer.

"Pfaw! Bird-watching is for fools," Boris snorts to himself, scrabbling back down. "I'm going inside for breakfast."

"House of Elegant French Kitten"

Finding no coffee in the kitchen of Laurent the Chartreux, Greta sighs dramatically and decides to look at the view from the roof herself. Immediately she spies a delicious bird!

"**mew!** Help! Boris! Help me capture the delicious bird!" she calls, but Boris is in the kitchen with Minnie, arguing over a bite of *boeuf bourguignon* they've found in the cardboard icebox.

"It's time to go," Boris announces when they are all three together in the Chartreux's kitchen. Sometimes he acts so bossy! He licks a dot of stew from his whisker and tucks his paw out the front door.

"First I will check to see if it's raining," he says.

"It is *not* raining. Let's go!!"

"Okaaaay," Minnie says tiredly.

"But I'm *so hungry.*

And we should take a nap pretty soon."

"Stop whining!" snaps Greta. "We need to get coffee. Maybe they'll have some at the firehouse."

Some like it HOT

MANY CATS LIVE AT THE FIREHOUSE: American Shorthairs, Manxes, even a Norwegian Forest Cat! They are strong and ready to work. But because Boxville Sur la Mer is made from cardboard, matches are outlawed in the town. There are never any fires!

Firemen without any fires to put out spend most of their time rescuing kittens from trees; but the kittens in the Boxville Sur la Mer fire brigade spend a lot of time *climbing* trees. They scale the trees to the highest branches and mew and mew! Then they have to rescue themselves—and they always do.

"Drat," Minnie reports after a quick tour of the empty firehouse. "They must be out climbing trees. The omelet pan is soaking in the sink. But they didn't leave any breakfast for us at all!"

"This is too much," moans Greta. Her eyes are glassy. "Look at me. I need coffee! I'm hallucinating. I see spots in front of my eyes!!"

"Those are bumblebees, stupid," scoffs Boris.

"Oh! They are? Oh! Yes! They're cute!"

"Oooooooooh, I'm dyyyyyyyyyying," wails Greta, clinging to the firehouse roof. "Do you think if I climb up here and call loudly to the fire brigade, they'll come home and make us some coffee?"

"Stop being so dramatic!" Boris swats Greta on the ear and briskly walks away. "Let's just go to the restaurant and get some coffee there. Maybe then you will finally stop complaining. For crying out loud!"

"You said they didn't have any coffee!"

Boris acts like he has not heard and trots away with his tail straight up. Minnie follows close behind him, muttering excitedly about biscuits.

"Grr," says Greta to herself, and out loud she cries, "Fine!" over her shoulder. She clambers down to run after her roommates. "But you are paying for my coffee, you lying little furball!"

please SEAT YOURSELF!

THE RESTAURANT IS OWNED BY A GINGER TOM named Pauly Pancakes. Some call him "Pauly" and some call him "Pancakes"— Pauly doesn't mind either way. Pauly tells everyone that he is "big boned," and most kittens sniff, "Oh, please!" when he says this, and roll their eyes at him, but not Minnie the Maine Coon—she understands. "Maine Coons sometimes get to be *twenty pounds*," she is known to say confidently to Pauly Pancakes, and they both will sit together at a table in the corner, nodding wisely at each other. "It's a known fact!"

Today, of course, Pauly Pancakes is on vacation, and the kitchen of the restaurant is quiet and still. Minnie sits in front of the cold stove and pouts. "If Pauly were here he would make us some breakfast," she says sullenly, watching Boris from the corner of her eye as he tries, without success, to scratch open the pantry door. "He keeps crackers and stuff in here!" huffs Boris. "Tinned fish!!"

"Oh, this is *ridiculous*," Greta groans, wandering out to the patio and casting her eyes heavenward. "Is there no coffee for me anywhere in this town?!"

"We *shall* have our coffees!" Boris shouts to his wilting roommate. A born showman, Boris identifies this moment as a perfect opportunity to display his considerable talents to Greta and Minnie, who sometimes do not share his appreciation for the dramatic arts. Boris leaps to the restaurant's awninged rooftop, filled with a divine excitement! "FEAR NOT!" he cries. "I shall perform the Dance of the Bringing of the Breakfasts!!"

"O°°°°°°°°°h Great Spirit of the Breakfast!"

(pounce)

"Bring unto us vast fishes and milks!!"

(roll)

"I offer to you this sacrifice of my
Gray Tabby roommate! Ha-ha!!"

35

"You better knock it off and get down from there," Greta says sharply.

"You are messing the place up! *Stop it!*" chirps Minnie, straightening the sign over the door. "It's not nice to disturb Pauly's restaurant. We should go." She prowls around the perimeter to make sure everything looks as clean and nice as when they arrived.

"Whatever," grumbles Boris, climbing down from the awning. "I can do the dance on the ground, too, you know. It's just *better* on the roof."

boris has low blood sugar, and sometimes it makes him act a little strange.

"Greeeeeeeeeeeeeeat Spirit of the Breakfast," he murmurs, rolling lazily on the ground outside the restaurant. He tries to concentrate on his dance, but it's hard not to be distracted by the tasty-looking clouds sneaking past, foggy fins flapping and wispy tails waving. "You guys," Boris calls. "You remember that kitty who was telling us about a cloudfish? You—hey! Are you listening? You think that was for real?" Greta and Minnie aren't listening, though. They have their heads bent together and are mourning their empty kitten tummies.

"Maybe my sister is home," Boris finally says, still lying on his back. He sighs, watching delicious birds fly far above his cardboard town. They are very far out of his reach. "She will have something good to eat, I bet. Maybe . . . a delicious fish . . ."

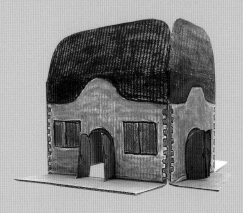

mi casa de carton
ES SU CASA DE CARTON*

BORIS'S SISTER LIVES DOWN THE STREET in a small Italian-style cottage. She says it is "rustic," but Boris likes to remind her that "rustic" is not the same thing as "totally messy all of the time."

By now Boris is so punchy that he does not even mind when he enters the cottage to find that his sister, like everyone else in Boxville Sur la Mer, is not at home, sitting by a sunny window and waiting to make breakfast for them all. Greta and Minnie climb into chairs at either end of the bare dining table, and they mew and cry and put their tiny heads in their tiny paws and howl with tiny despair. But Boris merely bustles through the house, humming. He fluffs the houseplants and adds a few special scratches to the arm of his sister's couch. "Better," he nods. Opening the doors and shutters wide, he says brightly, "Isn't it stuffy in here! What a house my sister keeps, eh girls?"

"We're hungry," Minnie reminds him, sulking.

"And sleepy," yawns Greta. She mews pitifully and puts her head down on the dining table. She is almost ready to give up on her dream of coffee.

* *"My Cardboard House Is Your Cardboard House"*

But Boris **will not** give up! "I know what to do!"
he yells, darting out the door and calling to the sleepy girls
as he goes.

"Probably my sister took the kids next door, to our mom's house!
We can have a *fantastic* breakfast there!

"Waffles!

"Kippers!

"Anything you want! My mom will make it for us! Come on!!"

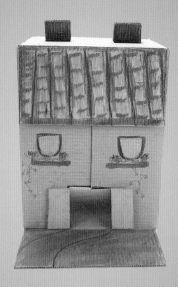

m°m's VILLA

AS YOU HAVE PROBABLY GUESSED ALREADY, Boris's mother and sister are nowhere to be found within the lovely Mediterranean manor next door. There is, though, a bowl of goldfish crackers on the kitchen table, and next to it a note for Boris:

> *Boris, my darling,*
> *Your sister and I have taken the baby kittens to the aquarium to see the delicious fishes. Please join us there if you would like, or, if not, perhaps we can meet for lunch afterward at the café? Bring your adorable friends Greta and Minnie! Such sweet girls!*
>
> *All my love,*
> *Mama*
>
> *P.S. Don't fill up on those goldfish, they're only meant for a snack!*

"Your mom is nice," Minnie says, her mouth crowded with tiny crackers.

"Awwwww, Mama," purrs Boris, rolling in the front doorway. "She *is* nice. Let's go to the aquarium and see her."

"No . . . we should just stay here—and make some coffee,"
Greta says anxiously. "I think it's going to rain."

"It surely won't rain," says Minnie,
settling down comfortably.
"But maybe we should take a nap,
and consider it?"

"Yes," Greta says, tapping her paws together
with great nervousness.
"I think it certainly will rain."

Boris feels confused, staring up
at the sunny sky, but on the other hand,
taking a little nap in his mother's house
sounds so very cozy just now.

BRUNCH, LUNCH, a pleasant kitty-chat

"MY CAFÉ IS OOOOOOOOPEN . . ." croons Celia the Siamese.
All morning she has been waiting for kittens to come in and
order hot coffee and fish-flavored pastries, but all morning
she has been lonesome.

"I have delicious coffee . . ."

Celia climbs to the roof of her café, purring quietly and observing
the insects on the sidewalk below. *I could catch them if I wanted to,* she
thinks. But she lets the insects walk past.

"Smoked salmon with buckwheat blini . . ."

Celia climbs down and crawls inside her café. "See how cozy the
café is!" she calls out to Boxville Sur la Mer, but all kittens of
Boxville Sur la Mer are sleeping, or on holiday, or out hunting, or
touring the aquarium. "I have hot chocolate and warm milk with
honey, too . . .!"

Celia licks her paw delicately and preens her ears.

"Half price on goat cheese quiche."

"As you can see from my quaint sign, my café
is open—if you want to come in, just ask!
Tap me on the back, and I will remove myself
from the doorway, no problem at all."

"If you feel cold or you are worried
that it will rain, I am happy to close
up the patio doors for your comfort."

"If you don't want to have any coffee,
we can just talk!"

farm FRESH

AS BORIS THE RUSSIAN BLUE NAPS IN THE VILLA, and Celia the Siamese polishes her espresso machine, Malcolm the Scottish Fold keeps a vigilant eye on his farm. He has heard the commotion of Boris's theatrics down the street and is poised to avert any similar disturbance in his own yard.

"Aye, those wee kitties are nowt but scoundrels, the lot of 'em," Malcolm mutters to himself. "They cannae be still fer even a minna!"

It seems to the casual observer that Malcolm is always cranky, but really he's only cranky about half the time. It's not his fault that his ears are flat on his head like that—he looks annoyed even when he isn't! Also, in all fairness to Malcolm, it's true that kittens often come uninvited to his farm, and eat all the eggs, and drink all the milk, and scare all the chickens, and bite all the cardboard machinery. It is hard to run a farm in a town full of hungry and playful kitties.

"I ha'nt come to *yer* homes without I was invited!"

Malcolm continues to stand over his property, growling and muttering for kitties to stay away, even though no one is nearby to hear him, only Celia, humming in her café at the other end of town.

FISH *Story*

WHAT MIGHT SURPRISE YOU about Malcolm the cranky Scottish Fold is that he has a sweet and pretty wife, also a Scottish Fold, who is not cranky at all and loves wee kitties. She is a teacher at the preschool down the road. At the preschool, the tiniest kittens of Boxville Sur la Mer begin their education. Here they learn colors, numbers, and shapes; how to mew at the door when they want to play outside; and how to wait until no one is looking before jumping onto the counter to eat the butter.

The baby kittens also learn about all the different fish! As everyone already knows, Boxville Sur la Mer has the best aquarium of any cardboard town in the world—cats come from near and far to study the plentiful and diverse marine life along the Boxville Sur la Mer coast. Many prominent cat marine biologists come from the University of Boxville Sur la Mer, and kitties are never too young to start learning about the strange, potentially delicious creatures in the ocean.

The baby kittens visit the aquarium several times each month, and they try hard to listen carefully as the scientist tells them all about the bluefin, the great white, the bell jelly, the rosy rockfish. It is hard to sit still for so long!

Like all little ones, baby kittens are very curious. They are always asking questions. Sometimes it drives you crazy!

"Where's my mama?"

"Is this the way to go to the aquarium?"

"Who lives in this cardboard house?"

"Why

do some cardboards
taste more delicious
than others?"

"Why do you always tell me,
'Don't jump onto the table'?"

"If I jump off this tabl
will you kitties catch m

"Are we almost to the aquarium?"

"DO YOU SEE THOSE ANTS ON THE GROUND?!"

"If we hide behind this house
do you think Mama will find us?"

"Are we lost?"

"Are you guys hiding
behind this house?"

"Where is everyone?!"

finally the kittens arrive at the aquarium on their field trip. First they stop at the visitor's center and wait while Mama Cat pays admission for the whole group. "Look at that cloud," mews Tiny Mickey. "It is shaped like a fish! Maybe we will see a cloudfish inside. If we see one, I will sneak in here later and catch it and eat it! You watch me. I can do it. I'm not afraid."

"Pssh, there's no such thing as a cloudfish," says Tiny Nicky, rolling her eyes. "You don't know anything."

"Well my cousin says there *is*," Tiny Mickey growls. "He saw one. He ate it! It was delicious! He ate six of them! He ate a hundred!"

"He did not," says Tiny Nicky. She is feeling sleepy.

"There's a *sun*fish and a *star*fish," Tiny Mickey says, running in an excited circle. "I don't see why there can't be a *cloud*fish, too. I heard it is the most delicious fish there ever was! It's so delicious you never want to eat another fish ever again!"

"There's no cloudfishes! Please," yawns Tiny Nicky, settling down in the doorway of the visitor's center and closing her eyes. "It's just nonsense. There's a *clown*fish," she allows. She's acting like such a know-it-all!

"*You're* a clownfish!!"

"Zzz," says Tiny Nicky.

Inside the aquarium the baby kittens see whales, sharks, jellyfish, crabs, bat rays, and even a giant octopus, but no cloudfish. Tiny Mickey says this is because cloudfish only live in the sky. "They would melt in this water," he insists, watching a moray eel swim past his fluffy face.

"Right," says Tiny Nicky lazily.

But later, when the field trip is over, Tiny Nicky looks into the sky, and for a few seconds she notices the unmistakable shape of a delicious fish in the cloud above her. The cloud wiggles its fuzzy fin and swims off into the blue.

"Oh my gosh! Tiny Mickey was right!!" gasps Tiny Nicky to herself. And she runs home as fast as her tiny legs will take her, to ask her mama if they can have cloudfish for dinner.

So goes a typical day in Boxville Sur la Mer! As you now may understand, though the outlandish myth of Boxville Sur la Mer prevails, the real lives of kitties here are not so different from your life, or mine—except for being so very much cuter. It is hard sometimes not to wish you could stay forever, but trust me, you cannot! So much fluffiness and coziness and precious purring all day long is only healthy for a kitten, and that's why only kittens live in Boxville Sur la Mer. It's nothing personal!

And so, gentle visitor, I see that your tour of Boxville Sur la Mer has come to an end this day as well. But don't be sad! Maybe you had hoped to visit the arcade and challenge Boris's high score on Cardboard Frogger, or perhaps you meant to tiptoe through the special collections room of the Boxville Sur la Mer Public Library, perusing some rare and bitable cardboard books. You can come back anytime!

Although you cannot live here in a cute cardboard house, it's okay to visit whenever you want. All kitties of Boxville Sur la Mer will be glad to see you again. If they seem like they are not interested to see you, and they are staring up into the sky and they don't answer when you say, "Hi! Kitty!" don't be offended. You know how clever the kittens of Boxville Sur la Mer are, and probably they are just trying to figure out how to catch a cloud-fish for their supper.